CW00726464

Contents

Foreword

The NHS needs leadership of the highest calibre if it is to respond successfully to financial and service pressures that are unprecedented in its history. In previous reports, The King's Fund has argued that we need to move on from a concept of heroic leaders who turn around organisational performance to seeing leadership as shared and distributed throughout the NHS. The Fund has also argued that leaders must engage their colleagues and other stakeholders in bringing about improvements in patient care and transforming the way in which care is provided.

In these new reports prepared with the Center for Creative Leadership (CCL), we build on previous work to make the case for collective leadership as the key to unlocking cultural change throughout the NHS. The reports both describe what collective leadership is and outline the key components of a collective leadership strategy. They draw on the combined expertise of staff at the Fund and CCL with the aim of supporting NHS organisations to move beyond high-level concepts to put in place the practical actions needed to develop and strengthen leadership from the board to the front lines of care delivery.

The reports make clear that responsibility for developing a collective leadership strategy rests firmly with the boards of NHS organisations. Every board must ensure that it understands the leadership capabilities required in future, how these are going to be developed and acquired, and what organisational and leadership interventions will enable them to be delivered. The CQC have echoed this in their new framework for well-led organisations. This process of discovery, design and delivery can help to develop the collective leadership needed in NHS organisations in order to deliver care that is safe, of high quality and within budget.

The bigger prize is to put in place the collective leadership needed to transform how health and care are delivered across local health systems. This requires organisations to develop individuals and teams able to work collaboratively for the greater good of the populations they serve. At a time when there is growing interest in integrated care and partnership working between the NHS, local authorities and third sector organisations, collective leadership in local health systems has never been more important or necessary.

While work to develop collective leadership must start now, time will be needed to turn the concepts into action. The King's Fund and CCL will be supporting the NHS to translate and adapt the thinking in these reports as organisations and systems seek to build the capabilities needed in future. Only when this happens will the NHS truly be able to tap into the skills, motivation and commitment that the 1.4 million people they employ bring to their work every day, and on which high-quality care for patients depends.

Chris Ham
Chief Executive
The King's Fund

David Altman
Executive Vice-President
CCL-EMEA

This paper is a collaboration between the Center for Creative Leadership and The King's Fund.

The Center for Creative Leadership and The King's Fund are currently developing an offer to support NHS organisations in the design of a collective leadership strategy. For more information please contact:

Kathryn Kernick
Regional Director UK and Ireland
Center for Creative Leadership
kernickk@ccl.org

Nicola Hartley
Director, Leadership Development
The King's Fund
n.hartley@kingsfund.org.uk

The Center for Creative Leadership (CCL) is a 501 (c) (3) non-profit educational institution, headquartered in Greensboro, North Carolina, US. It is a top-ranked, global provider of leadership development. By leveraging the power of leadership to drive results that matter most to clients, CCL transforms individual leaders, teams, organisations and society. Its array of cutting-edge solutions is steeped in extensive research and experience gained from working with hundreds of thousands of leaders at all levels.

Key messages

- The most important determinant of the development and maintenance of an organisation's culture is current and future leadership. Every interaction by every leader at every level shapes the emerging culture of an organisation.

- Boards are responsible for ensuring their organisation develops a coherent, effective and forward-looking collective leadership strategy for their organisation and assuring themselves that it is implemented. This strategy comes from purposefully describing the leadership culture desired for that organisation.

- Collective leadership means everyone taking responsibility for the success of the organisation as a whole – not just for their own jobs or work area. This contrasts with traditional approaches to leadership, which have focused on developing individual capability while neglecting the need for developing collective capability or embedding the development of leaders within the context of the organisation they are working in.

- Collective leadership cultures are characterised by all staff focusing on continual learning and, through this, on the improvement of patient care. It requires high levels of dialogue, debate and discussion to achieve shared understanding about quality problems and solutions.

- Leaders need to ensure that all staff adopt leadership roles in their work and take individual and collective responsibility for delivering safe, effective, high-quality and compassionate care for patients and service users. Achieving this requires careful planning, persistent commitment and a constant focus on nurturing leadership and culture.

Context and culture

The NHS is confronted by radically changing demographic pressures and hugely increasing demands. Alongside these is the need to build public confidence after several high-profile scandals, to increase productivity and to promote innovation in health and social care. This all comes as public sector financial cuts are implemented on a large scale.

How can health care organisations respond effectively to these challenges? Policy-makers, academics, patient leaders and practitioners, when posed this question repeatedly identify organisational culture as central to the effectiveness of health care organisations.

Culture is a set of shared, taken-for-granted implicit assumptions that members of an organisation hold and that determines how they perceive, think about and react to things (Schein 1992). In other words, it is 'the way we do things around here'. Every interaction in an organisation both reveals and shapes its culture – for instance, how staff talk to or about patients, and how they talk to each other. Culture reflects what an organisation values: quality, safety, productivity, survival, power, secrecy, justice, humanity and so on. If there are strong values of compassion and safety, new staff learn the importance of caring and safe practice. If they observe senior staff behaving aggressively or brusquely, they assimilate that. In short, if we want to improve care, we must focus on nurturing appropriate cultures.

Cultures are co-created by all in the organisation and they are dynamic. This is because individuals within organisations are constantly communicating, influencing, collaborating and competing up, down and across the organisation. This constant activity creates the cultures that exist within specialties, directorates, organisations and whole systems.

But the most important determinant of the development and maintenance of cultures is current and future leadership (Schneider and Barbera 2014). Leaders have the power to reward and punish; they control information and resources; they make choices about structure; and they shape the work lives of others for better or worse. Leaders therefore command much of our attention. We note what they value – what they pay attention to, monitor, reward and reinforce. By doing so, we learn the values we must adopt to win leaders' approval. The followers of positive, supportive leaders behave more co-operatively and empathically.

Therefore NHS organisations must be led consciously and carefully to reinforce values of high-quality care that permeate their organisations, from top to bottom and end to end. But this does not happen by chance or by focusing only on individual leadership development.

Collective leadership: a basis for caring cultures

Collective leadership represents a new way of sharing power, ensuring that leadership and expertise are correlated at every level in relation to every task. It also represents a strategy for integrating leadership collectively across the organisation. The ultimate responsibility for the quality of care provided by an organisation rests with NHS boards. Effective boards ensure their organisation has a continually evolving and clearly articulated leadership strategy designed to develop and sustain a culture of high-quality care. The Care Quality Commission (CQC) now recognises competence in this regard by incorporating into its inspections key lines of enquiry on whether organisations are well led. A component of this is the extent to which boards have ensured a leadership strategy is in place. And Monitor's 2014–17 strategy involves paying more attention to the capabilities of provider organisations to make the changes necessary for providing integrated care (Monitor 2014). This includes making sure that system leaders are working together effectively, nationally and locally – in effect, that there is collective leadership at every level.

Collective leadership means the distribution and allocation of leadership power to wherever expertise, capability and motivation sit within organisations. The purposeful, visible distribution of leadership responsibility onto the shoulders of every person in the organisation is vital for creating the type of collective leadership that will nurture the right culture for health care (McCauley 2011). In such a culture, roles of leadership and 'followership' shift depending on situational requirements. Collective leadership creates the culture in which high-quality, compassionate care can be delivered.

At a system level, collective leadership cultures for high-quality, compassionate care reach beyond the boundaries of specific organisations. They provide the basis for the creation of such cultures across the whole system, forging an interdependent network of organisations that work together to deliver high-quality care. In recognising that organisations cannot work in isolation to achieve the best possible care, it follows that their cultures need to be conducive to interdependent working within and across the system. This is a core argument for collective leadership.

A collective leadership strategy emerges from a conscious and intelligent effort to plan for an integrated, collective network of leaders, including patients, distributed throughout the organisation and embodying shared values and practices (Browning *et al* 2011; The King's Fund 2011). The aim of the strategy must be to create a leadership community in which all staff take responsibility for nurturing cultures of high-quality and compassionate care. The strategy should require all staff to prioritise the effectiveness of the organisation and sector as a whole in creating this culture, rather than focusing only on individual or team success. Every member of staff has the potential to lead at many points in time, particularly when their expertise is relevant to the task in hand. It is also important to ensure all staff are focused on good followership, regardless of their seniority in the organisation.

To achieve this, senior leaders must understand the leadership practices and behaviours needed to nurture a caring culture. Understanding culture alone is insufficient; conscious, deliberate attention must be paid to enabling people at every level within the organisation to adopt leadership practices that nurture the cultures the NHS requires. For collective, distributed leadership (and followership), all staff must be engaged.

Leadership for cultures of high-quality care

The reports of the inquiries into the scandals, tragedies and problems of NHS organisations, such as in the Mid Staffordshire NHS Trust and Winterbourne View, identified organisational cultures as fundamental. The values and normative behaviours in those situations created the conditions for what ensued.

The components of good care – improving quality, increasing productivity, nurturing compassion, ensuring effectiveness, stimulating innovation and sustaining patient satisfaction – can be achieved only where the cultures of organisations are underpinned by the core values of the NHS – compassion, dignity, respect and equality, with high-quality care the overriding value. These create the conditions most associated with organisational cultures that encourage innovation, quality improvement and learning (National Advisory Group on the Safety of Patients in England 2013).

What cultural characteristics are fundamental for the delivery of continually improving high-quality care? Key cultural characteristics:

- are an inspiring vision and compelling strategic narrative

- have associated clear objectives and priorities at every level from board to front line

- have supportive people management and leadership

- have high levels of staff engagement and therefore the conditions that lead to staff engagement

- learning and innovation the responsibility of all

- have high levels of genuine team working and co-operation across boundaries.

How does collective leadership nurture these characteristics?

The top priority is for leaders at every level to communicate an inspiring, forward-looking and ambitious vision focused on offering high-quality, compassionate care to the communities they serve. Good leaders reiterate the message at every level that such care is the core purpose of all staff (Dixon-Woods *et al* 2013), so that everyone understands and acts on this commitment. This takes time, sustained energy and persistent commitment.

Staff in health services report that they are often overwhelmed by their workload and unclear about their priorities (Dixon-Woods *et al* 2013). This produces stress, inefficiency and poor-quality care. This can arise from too many priorities raining down from senior managers. Vision and mission statements about high-quality, compassionate care provide a directional path for staff. But they must be translated into clear, aligned, agreed and challenging objectives at all levels of the organisation, from the board to frontline teams and individuals (Locke and Latham 2013). Agreeing clear objectives is the most important element of effective appraisals for staff in terms of performance. This must be matched by timely, helpful and formative feedback for those delivering care if they are to improve continually the quality of care.

If we want staff to treat patients with respect, care and compassion, all leaders and staff must treat their colleagues with respect, care and compassion. Directive, aggressive or brusque leaders dilute the ability of staff to make good decisions, deplete their emotional resources and hinder their ability to relate effectively to patients, especially those who are most distressed or difficult. There are also clear links between staff experience and patient outcomes. Staff views of their leaders are strongly related to patients' perceptions of the quality of care. The higher the levels of satisfaction and commitment that staff report, the higher the levels of satisfaction patients report. When staff report high levels of supportiveness from their immediate managers, patients report receiving better care. If leaders and managers create positive, supportive environments for staff, the staff in turn create caring, supportive environments and deliver higher-quality care for patients. Such leadership cultures encourage staff engagement.

Staff engagement in health services refers to an experience of work that is involving, at times exciting, meaningful, energising, affirming, stretching and connecting.

It is characterised by strong identification with the organisation and a drive to be involved in decision-making and innovation to improve the delivery of care. Data from the UK National Staff Survey reveal that staff engagement trumps all other measures (staff satisfaction, leadership, human resource management (HRM) practices) as the best overall predictor of NHS organisations' outcomes. It predicts patient mortality (in the acute sector), care quality and financial performance (based on CQC ratings), patient satisfaction, and staff absenteeism, health and wellbeing across all sectors. Leaders help create the conditions for high staff engagement by:

- promoting a positive climate

- recognising staff contributions

- providing information

- giving helpful feedback

- supporting staff innovation

- promoting fairness and transparency

- developing trusting relationships.

Sustaining cultures of high-quality care involves all staff focusing on continual learning and improvement of patient care, 'top to bottom and end to end', and thereby taking leadership responsibility for improving quality (National Advisory Group on the Safety of Patients in England 2013). The same applies to staff 'continually and forever reducing harm'; ensuring reflective practice is endemic and taking responsibility for giving both positive and negative feedback on safety behaviours to colleagues (regardless of seniority). Where there is a culture of collective leadership, all staff members are likely to intervene to solve problems, to ensure quality of care and to promote responsible, safe innovation. Collective leadership focused on improvement should ensure that:

- teams at all levels collectively take time out to review and improve their performance

- mastery of quality and patient safety sciences and practices is an ongoing priority for all

- there are high levels of dialogue, debate and discussion across the organisation (top to bottom and end to end) to achieve shared understanding about quality problems and solutions.

This is what collective leadership implies. Similarly, all staff will encourage, welcome and explore feedback and treat complaints and errors as opportunities for system learning rather than as a prompt for blame. This encourages collective openness to and learning from errors, near misses and incidents.

Cultures of quality and safety require a strong value of team-working. Health care staff, across professional boundaries, have to work interdependently to provide high-quality and safe care for patients (Lyubovnikova and West 2013; West 2012). Where multi-professional teams work together, patient satisfaction is higher, health care delivery is more effective, there are higher levels of innovation in the provision of new and improved ways of caring for patients, lower levels of staff stress, absenteeism and turnover, and more consistent communication with patients. Leadership that ensures effective team and inter-team working (both within and across organisational boundaries) is essential if NHS organisations are to meet the challenges ahead. Shared leadership in teams is a strong predictor of team performance (D'Innocenzo *et al* 2014).

As the Francis Inquiry and Berwick reports emphasise, creating such cultures requires a conscious, collective approach to ensuring that the right leadership is in place to nurture the right values with the right behaviours. This requires a collective leadership strategy.

Collective leadership at Salford Royal: a model for quality improvement

Salford Royal NHS Foundation Trust established a vision to become the safest organisation in the NHS. It has achieved this by aspiring to provide safe, clean and personal care to every patient, every time. The chief executive has been in post for more than 12 years (compared with the two-year average tenure for chief executives). The organisation has a comprehensive quality improvement (QI) strategy and the board decides every year what to improve, by how much and by when. There is particular emphasis on making QI information available and accessible for all staff members, empowering them to take the lead in initiatives for their areas. Driver diagrams identify the primary and secondary drivers of improvement, and staff directly initiate and sustain improvements, supported by in-house QI experts. Learning from others both inside and outside the organisation is championed, exemplified by the establishment of NHS Quest, a network of 14 NHS organisations focused on cross-organisational learning for QI. Salford tracks QI performance and compares performance with that of other NHS organisations, for instance, on hospital standardised mortality ratios (HSMRs), readmissions and harms. The trust openly displays data on safety and quality in each ward (for example, on infections and falls) as well as information on required and actual staffing levels. Every bed has a white board beside it on which patients and family members can record what matters to them.

The executive team models the kind of leadership behaviour that emphasises core NHS values: they do patient safety walkabouts to identify and understand problems and spot examples of good care. They have set up charters of commitment with medical staff and between management and clinical staff, which have been hugely influential in changing the culture.

Leadership values and behaviours were developed with full staff engagement. In order to select, develop and retain the right people for a collective leadership culture, the organisation uses the GE 9-box grid to assess leaders' performance and potential. This helps decision-making on succession placement, readiness for promotion and attrition risk. Salford has a clear and transparent goal-setting and appraisal system that feeds into the organisation's vision, mission and strategic priorities.

As a result, Salford is in the top 10 per cent of trusts for performance on mortality rates; has good financial performance; and has good performance on the safety thermometer and on infections, falls and pressure ulcers. It has the highest consistent ratings on service quality. The National Staff Survey results for November 2013 reveal that Salford has the highest engagement scores in England for all NHS provider organisations. It also has the highest scores on many of the key findings within the survey, including staff satisfaction; being able to recommend the trust as a place to work or be treated; staff feeling satisfied with the quality of work and level of patient care they are able to offer; communication; support from immediate managers; team-working; and the proportion of staff reporting that they receive well-structured appraisals.

⑤ What is collective leadership?

In collective leadership cultures, responsibility and accountability function simultaneously at both individual and collective levels. They breed regular reflective practice focused on failure, exploratory learning and making continuous improvement an organisational habit. By contrast, command-and-control leadership cultures invite the displacement of responsibility and accountability onto single individuals, leading to scapegoating and creating a climate of fear of failure rather than an appetite for innovation.

Leadership comes from both the leaders themselves and the relationships among them. Organisational performance does not rest simply on the number or quality of individual leaders. What counts is the extent to which formal and informal leaders work collectively in support of the organisation's goals and in embodying the values that underpin the desired culture. Leadership also incorporates the concept of followership – everyone supporting each other, including leaders, to deliver high-quality care, and everyone taking responsibility for the success of the organisation as a whole.

Research and practice from the Center for Creative Leadership and The King's Fund show that, where leaders and leadership relationships are well developed, trusts will benefit from direction, alignment and commitment (Drath *et al* 2008; The King's Fund 2013, 2012). Direction refers to the agreement among people on what the organisation is working together to achieve (in other words, the organisational purpose). It includes goals and targets, for example about care quality and safety, as well as the organisation's mission and values, such as compassion, transparency, engagement and patient focus. Alignment refers to the effective co-ordination and integration of different aspects of the work so that everyone's efforts fit together in service of a shared commitment to patients. Commitment implies that everyone takes responsibility and works towards the success of the organisation as a whole as a priority.

There is also increasing recognition of the importance of new leadership coalitions with patients. The King's Find report *Patient-centred leadership* (2013) recommends that 'patient leaders should work alongside NHS leaders to support the transformation called for in the Francis Inquiry report.' Organisations such as the Centre for Patient Leadership also stress the importance of seeing patient leaders as a resource for change in health and social care organisations.[1] Much like multidisciplinary team-working, collective leadership with patients would require a redistribution of power and decision-making along with a shift in thinking about who is included in the collective leadership community. This is an emerging field and The King's Fund is currently developing an offer of help to organisations to develop this collective leadership and, thereby, the cultures that health care needs.

Collective leadership at Wrightington, Wigan and Leigh NHS Foundation Trust: empowering dialogue

The journey to staff engagement at Wrightington, Wigan and Leigh (WWL) NHS Foundation Trust began 15 years ago, as a joint initiative between senior managers and staff to increase mutual understanding and bridge hierarchical divides. Directors' 'walkabouts' give them the opportunity to listen to staff at the front line, and give staff regular opportunities to talk directly to the senior team. This engagement is greatly strengthened by the implementation of the Listening into Action (LiA) programme, which involves large-scale staff listening events led by the chief executive and other directors. Staff are asked three questions: what works well, what needs to improve, and what are the barriers to improvement? Getting these events ingrained in the trust's culture has produced quick wins and bigger system changes. They exemplify the opportunity for all staff to lead in the organisation.

A team-focused practice of collective leadership is the 'Pioneer Teams' programme, with staff running their own listening events and implementing local changes to improve services. The trust is working in partnership with Unipart to develop lean ways of working through team communication cells, and visual management tools, with the use of metrics and devolved problem-solving. Teams are encouraged to come together for 15 minutes daily to determine priorities, provide updates and address problems, and to recognise and appreciate successes. They record their progress visually at a central point to keep the whole team updated.

---

1. See *Bring it on,* a paper produced by the Centre for Patient Leadership and FPM for NHS Midlands and East for useful summary of the issues and practice of patient leadership and also a starting definition of who patient leaders are
http://centreforpatientleadership.com/wp-content/uploads/2013/04/Bring-it-on-40-ways-to-support-Patient-Leadership-FINAL-V-APRIL-2013.pdf

The key components of success are:

- a partnership approach between staff and management

- strong promotion of collective leadership through staff engagement

- communication of information on engagement levels and linked improvements in service delivery throughout the organisation

- quick action after listening events to bring about change

- timely feedback to staff about achievements through a 'you said – we did' approach.

The trust is promoting engagement as a cultural value: rather than simply ticking the box on the leadership question 'Have we asked our staff?', leaders not only ask, they also listen, support and empower staff to lead implementation. For some, it required shifting mindsets to lead this way and to make more informed and collaborative decisions through staff involvement. But it was worth it. As a consequence, the trust has seen major sustained improvements in staff survey scores, sickness absence levels and expenditure on temporary staffing and many benefits for patients, including improvements in patient care. More information is in an online video: http://bit.ly/1dB2fwO

Developing a collective leadership strategy

A leadership strategy is the result of a process of consciously and purposefully describing the desired leadership culture; identifying the skills and behaviours needed at an individual and collective level to create the desired culture; and planning the identification, development and diversity of designated individual leaders needed to implement and sustain the desired leadership culture. A leadership strategy is thus a truly organisational effort to tackle leadership as a collective organisational responsibility. It views leadership development as a means of creating collective capability in the organisation and endorses the integration of leadership development with organisational development. This contrasts with much traditional leader development work, which has focused on developing individual capability while neglecting the need for developing collective capability or embedding the development of people within the context of the organisation they are working in.

A leadership strategy makes explicit:

- how many leaders a health and social care organisation needs

- of what kind

- in which positions

- with which skills and

- the way in which they should behave, individually and collectively, to achieve high-quality and compassionate care for patients and service users.

Simply filling all the leadership positions on an organisational chart will not produce the quality of leadership now required in health and social care. What matters is what those people do and how they relate to one another. The challenge of recruiting and retaining leaders at all levels must be recognised. There is a need for clinical leadership at every level; for leadership teams where clinical and non-clinical staff work together without fault lines and schisms; and for committed medical staff who are engaged and privileged participants.

Power, authority and influence operate through formal hierarchical organisational structures of executive directors, deputy directors, directorate heads and team leaders among others; and through informal systems of personal contacts, length of tenure in post, professional allegiances and so on. Therefore when planning leadership in the context of nurturing cultures it is important to include both those leaders with formal leadership roles and those influential leaders found in every part of an organisation or system.

Through developing collective leadership strategies, the cultures necessary for our current and future health care services can be nurtured. Previous publications from The King's Fund suggest how those strategies should be shaped. In 2011, *The future of leadership and management in the NHS: no more heroes* (The King's Fund 2011) argued that the model of 'heroic' leadership was outdated and instead required a 'shared leadership' model within and across many organisations. This involves developing the organisation and its teams across systems of care. In 2012, *Leadership and engagement for improvement in the NHS: together we can* (The King's Fund 2012) focused on the importance of employee engagement. It argued that, in times of crucial change, we need a highly motivated workforce with energy, ideas and commitment if we are to be successful. The report argued that leaders are pivotal in cultivating a strong culture of engagement for patients and staff and that leaders must work as a collective group to create and sustain cultures of engagement. The report *Patient-centered leadership: rediscovering our purpose* (The King's Fund 2013), published following the inquiry at Mid Staffordshire Hospital, stated that leadership development is essential for nurturing an organisational culture in which patients' needs come first and for ensuring that the values of patient-centred care are communicated and understood at all levels in health care organisations. It recommended that the NHS should focus on constancy of purpose, organisational and leadership stability, and on allowing sufficient time to work on the many factors that contribute to delivering high-quality care.

A leadership development plan flows from the strategy to contribute to achieving the desired future state. It is a process that is considered, contextual and informed by data and requires disciplined commitment and action. By implication, leadership development will be fundamentally contextualised in the culture and strategy of the organisation concerned. It will not be a process of training individuals in remote locations in an atomistic fashion.

Collective leadership development at Nottinghamshire Healthcare Trust

Nottinghamshire Healthcare Trust's 9,000 staff provide integrated health care across Leicestershire, Nottinghamshire and Yorkshire. The trust's growth and success in recent years are attributed to its collective leadership, based on all staff taking responsibility for leading the organisation. Distributed and situational leadership are at the heart of its culture and are achieved through an array of purposeful and strategic development efforts. One such effort is the leadership development programme Invest to Lead, which stretches five learning days over a course of five months. It involves senior staff and equal numbers of clinicians and staff from non-clinical services. By June 2014, 1,300 staff will have completed the programme.

Participants are told that they are accountable for developing appraisals, communication, team-working, team performance, prioritisation, problem-solving and decision-making. The trust reiterates that leadership is held by all employees. The programme reinforces the fact that the best outcomes for patients will be provided by teams that are well led, appraised effectively and which have had time to commit to setting objectives. Organisational development objectives are clearly communicated throughout the programme. They include:

- continuous improvements in patient and carer satisfaction, involvement, recovery and power

- embedding a positive culture

- meeting and exceeding regulatory standards

- developing partnerships with commissioners, members and stakeholders through proactive support for partnership-working

- ensuring service transformation/redesign, primary/secondary care development, urgent care and long-term condition management

- promoting integrated care

- increasing information quality and accuracy to support clinical and patient decision-making

- further enhancing distributed leadership, supervision, appraisal and team development.

The programme aims to challenge staff by asking them to take responsibility for managing and leading change. Aside from presenting information and leading dialogue, senior staff in the programme are considered on the same footing as other staff members, listening and learning throughout the programme, thereby offering a role model of the type of leadership the organisation wants to develop. The chief executive presents information on the likely trends in their 'markets' and also describes trends in regional and national policy, seeking to map the future for the organisation. Current achievements are celebrated and distributed and compassionate leadership is encouraged. Core organisational values are reinforced, including valuing the individual, the work of both clinical and non-clinical staff, and staff commitment to patients.

The Invest to Lead programme encourages all staff to demonstrate leadership among their work colleagues, in whatever role they perform. The programme aims to help staff 'identify personal ambitions, role model influence, ensure service improvement, and develop insight and impact for their patients, their teams and themselves'. (For more information, see: http://tinyurl.com/ogqwsxu)

The strategy process

The process of developing a collective leadership strategy must begin with the board since the scale of the change process and resources required demand complete commitment from the most senior leaders. It will eventually require the engagement of all key stakeholders and leaders throughout the organisation. The process involves seeking out, sensing, adopting and adapting good practice wherever it is found. This could be from both within and outside the NHS, from within the United Kingdom and abroad.

The detailed design phase begins with data collection to inform the organisation about its current state and to enable key stakeholders and design groups to sculpt the strategy. In organisations that have successfully developed collective leadership, the implementation of the strategy has been sustained and rigorous, with leaders at all levels showing courage and persistence. Consistent with an evidence-based approach to health care delivery, the strategy implementation process and key outcomes are evaluated at every step (see box). All systems within the organisation will support the collective leadership strategy. So, for example, HR practices will reinforce collective leadership approaches and core values through recruitment, induction, training, performance management and appraisal.

Collective leadership development at Southern Health: a strategy for sustainable culture change

Southern Health NHS Foundation Trust was formed in 2011 following the merger of Hampshire Partnership NHS Foundation Trust and Hampshire Community Health Care. Southern Health considers nurturing culture as critical for business performance given that quality of care, levels of safety, patient experience and efficiency are all shaped by culture. The trust has been explicit about the culture being sought by defining a set of values that underpin the behaviours required from all staff in the organisation. The focus of these efforts is on ensuring that service users receive ever-improving high-quality and compassionate health and social care. Partly inspired by Virgin Atlantic (Virgin Atlantic 2012), these values form the basis on which all staff and leaders are recruited, appraised and developed, including targeted leadership development for more than 1,000 leaders.

Southern Health has implemented assessment processes to ensure the right people get appointed, especially to leadership positions; behaviourally based appraisal to align all objectives to the business plan and all behaviours to values; talent management to identify, nurture and retain staff on the basis of their current performance and future potential; and succession-planning to identify those with the potential to move into leadership positions.

The organisation has used a variety of methods to develop internal leadership capability including:

- a programme to develop the leadership characteristics required for the business

- a focus on driving integration to achieve collective leadership

- communications that reinforce the principle that quality of care is everyone's top priority

- a coaching programme for leaders

- a tailored development intervention for the senior management team

- team development for newly formed teams or those facing challenges

- a value-based programme of induction for new medical consultants to support them in adjusting to a leadership role.

All of Southern Health's development programmes are specially designed to help nurture the culture, rather than being 'off the shelf' programmes.

To evaluate the collective leadership strategy, they gather data on cultural shift; assess the predictive validity of selection methods; measure shifts in leadership behaviours using ratings from 360° and values-based appraisals; and assess whether team and individual objectives are becoming significantly more challenging. Future strategies include developing the leadership of integrated teams to co-create services with patients, including providing support and development to those pivotal in driving system change and integration regardless of their employer; embedding the assessment and appraisal processes; extending talent management across the organisation; and providing targeted development to individuals and teams in the most critical leadership roles.

The collective leadership strategy focuses on the skills and behaviours that leaders will bring and develop to shape the desired culture. These will include generic behavioural competencies that apply to all leaders in the organisation, such as:

- compassion and supportiveness

- commitment to improving care

- effectively involving service users, patients and carers

- focusing on performance and ensuring accountability

- supporting innovation

- making intelligent use of data

- managing poor performance

- helping to solve systems problems.

They will also include specific behavioural competencies depending on the role the leader occupies, such as a specific clinical competence; understanding specific care quality indicators; budgetary competence.

The strategy will also specify the collective capabilities of leaders when acting together. These include:

- providing a sense of direction

- demonstrating alignment with departmental or service goals

- generating commitment as a collective leadership team to the success of the organisation overall

- proactively solving system problems or making improvements that require collaboration across internal or external departments or organisational boundaries (for example, improving co-ordination between community mental health teams)

- engaging all staff in dialogue and in decision-making processes and gaining their support in taking forward innovations

- jointly formulating approaches and problem-solving with leaders across the organisation and implementing them in a co-ordinated fashion (for example, dealing with slow discharge or communication problems between health and social care)

- implementing successful innovation requiring multidisciplinary and multi-agency collaboration (for example, improving the efficiency of patient pathways)

- adapting to change in a coherent, collective manner

- being responsive to patients and carers in a way that demonstrates shared responsibility.

There are significant challenges in leader recruitment: currently 10 per cent of chief executive roles are unfilled, and trusts struggle to fill many other senior leadership roles. This will require all leaders to develop talent on behalf of the organisation as a whole, rather than only for individual units.

Given the importance to services of appropriate diversity of leaders and equality and trust in health care organisations, the leadership strategy will determine the leadership characteristics required. This will include diversity of age, gender (most organisations have a dearth of women leaders at certain levels), race (the leadership of organisations should represent equality groups appropriately and the diversity of the populations they serve), culture of origin, education, experience, subject matter expertise (such as anaesthetics or HRM), and so on.

The strategy must also design systems and processes that ensure leaders work together effectively to nurture and sustain the desired culture via leadership teams. Leadership should address and solve systems problems, monitor collective leadership processes and engage in collective learning about their leadership.

The success of leadership strategy design and implementation depends on how the behaviours adopted by those undertaking the strategy development mirrors the behaviour described by the strategy. Role modelling is key.

7

Memorial Hospital: developing a collective leadership strategy

Memorial Hospital is a 600-bed teaching hospital in the United States. It has 4,200 staff and is recognised for its outstanding cardiac and oncological care (Brimmer 2012). Memorial faced a number of challenges including introducing integrated electronic medical records; the need for radical cost-cutting to meet Medicare break-even targets; resource-sharing among a number of organisations; and the establishment of accountable care alliances across health and social care organisations.

Developing the collective leadership strategy initially involved the strategic leadership team, management teams, the physician leadership team, physicians' teams, a change leadership team, 'trust teams' and the CEO. The teams met regularly during the planning and implementation two-year period. These meetings aimed to create space to discuss big ideas for improvement rather than simply being detail-focused committees. They tied leadership development directly to the hospital strategy; enabled everyone to be clear about what was required to succeed; justified expenditures of time, money and energy; clarified executive responsibilities for talent management; provided the context for talent management processes, systems and policies; and heightened the relevance and purpose of leadership.

There were three phases to the work.

- Phase 1 was an initial discovery process that included a review of the hospital's mission, vision, strategic plan, employee engagement and survey results, organisational documents, as well as interviews with senior leaders, focus groups, leadership surveys and organisational assessments.

- Phase 2 was a design process, focused on the senior leadership team including providing an overview of the leadership strategy work; data collection in real time; feedback and discussion on initial discovery data; current state/future state exploration and discussion; executive team learning; facilitated dialogue; and agreement on next steps. Identifying required leadership competencies and organisational capabilities was key to supporting the hospital strategy, along with a shared understanding of the culture that the hospital required. This was used to inform talent management and organisation design.

- Phase 3 was the application of the leadership strategy framework. This included facilitated organisational development such as the culture change programme, building team effectiveness, developing boundary spanning and dialogue; and individual leadership development incorporating leadership programmes (including 360° and other assessments), coaching, action learning and elearning.

Memorial Hospital saw an evolution from the view that 'leaders are people in authority', through 'leadership emerges out of individual expertise and heroic action' to the point where they aimed to see 'leadership is a collective activity'.

Leadership strategy started with the board, which then engaged other key leaders before developing both formal and informal leadership throughout the hospital. Fundamental to the change programme was the notion that individual and organisational leadership together create leadership culture. Individual leadership is what individual leaders must do; organisational leadership is what leaders across the organisation must do together.

8 Conclusions

For health care organisations to be good places in which to both work and receive compassionate, high-quality care, we need cultures that sustain high-quality care at multiple levels. These cultures:

- focus above all on the delivery of high-quality, safe health care

- enable staff to do their jobs effectively

- genuinely value, support and nurture 'the front line'

- ensure that there is a strong connection to the shared purpose, whatever one's role or position within the system

- ensure collaboration across professional, role and organisational boundaries

- achieve high staff engagement at all levels

- enable and support patient and service-user involvement

- are models of service-user responsiveness

- ensure transparency, openness and candor

- are places where people accept responsibility for outcomes, and welcome learning and innovation from errors or failures

- promote and value clinical leadership

- support, value and recognise staff

- are places where leaders create opportunities for others to lead

- exist where there is an overriding commitment to learning, improvement and innovation in all services at all levels.

Only an appropriate collective leadership culture, developed from a conscious and intelligent leadership strategy, can achieve all this. Our companion paper, *Delivering a collective leadership strategy for health care* (Eckert *et al* 2014), offers guidance to boards on the process of developing and implementing leadership strategies, in three key steps (discover, design, deliver). The challenges facing health care organisations are too great and too numerous for leadership to be left to chance or to piecemeal approaches. By working together with health and social care organisations to address this profoundly important issue, we can develop leadership strategies that will ensure they face the future with confidence and deliver the high-quality, compassionate care that is their mission.

References

Brimmer K (2012). 'Top 100 hospitals named by Thomson Reuters'. *Healthcare IT News*, 27 April. Available at: www.healthcareitnews.com/news/top-100-hospitals-named-thomson-reuters (accessed on 16 April 2014).

Browning HW, Torain DJ, Patterson TE (2011). *Collaborative health care leadership*. Greensboro, NC: Center for Creative Leadership.

D'Innocenzo L, Mathieu JE, Kukenberger MR (2014). 'A meta-analysis of different forms of shared leadership – team performance relations'. *Journal of Management*, published online Mar 10; doi10.1177/0149206314525205

Dixon-Woods M, Baker R, Charles K, Dawson J, Jerzembek G, Martin G, McCarthy I, McKee L, Minion J, Ozieranski P, Willars J, Wilkie P, West M (2013). 'Culture and behaviour in the English National Health Service: overview of lessons from a large multimethod study'. *British Medical Journal Quality and Safety*, vol 23, pp 106–15.

Drath WH, McCauley CD, Palus CJ, Van Velsor E, O'Connor PMG, McGuire JB (2008). 'Direction, alignment, commitment: toward a more integrative ontology of leadership'. *Leadership Quarterly*, vol 19, 635–53.

Eckert R, West M, Altman D, Steward K, Pasmore B (2014). *Delivering a collective leadership strategy for health care*. Greensboro, NC: Center for Creative Leadership and The King's Fund. Available at: www.kingsfund.org.uk/collectiveleadershipdelivery (accessed on 12 May 2104).

Locke EA, Latham GP (2013). *New developments in goal setting and task performance*. New York: Routledge.

Lyubovnikova J, West MA(2013). 'Why teamwork matters: enabling health care team effectiveness for the delivery of high quality patient care' in Salas E, Tannembaum SI, Cohen D, Latham G (eds), *Developing and enhancing teamwork in organizations*, pp 331–72. San Francisco: Jossey Bass.

McCauley C (2011). *Making leadership happen*. Greensboro, NC: Center for Creative Leadership.

Monitor (2014). *Monitor's strategy 2014–17: helping to redesign healthcare provision in England*. London: Monitor.

National Advisory Group on the Safety of Patients in England (2013). *A promise to learn – a commitment to act: improving the safety of patients in England*. London: Department of Health. Available at: www.gov.uk/government/publications/berwick-review-into-patient-safety (accessed on 15 April 2014).

Pasmore W (2013). *Developing a leadership strategy.* Greensboro, NC: Center for Creative Leadership.

Schein E (1992). *Organizational culture and leadership.* San Francisco: Jossey Bass.

Schneider B, Barbera KM (eds) (2014). *Oxford handbook of organizational climate and culture.* New York: Oxford University Press.

The King's Fund (2013). *Patient-centred leadership: rediscovering our purpose.* London: The King's Fund. Available at: www.kingsfund.org.uk/publications/patient-centred-leadership (accessed on 16 April 2014).

The King's Fund (2012). *Leadership and engagement for improvement in the NHS: together we can.* London: The King's Fund. Available at: www.kingsfund.org.uk/publications/leadership_review_12.html (accessed on 16 April 2014).

The King's Fund (2011). *The future of leadership and management in the NHS: no more heroes.* Report from The King's Fund Commission on Leadership and Management in the NHS. Available at: www.kingsfund.org.uk/publications/future-leadership-and-management-nhs (accessed on 16 April 2014).

Virgin Atlantic (2012). 'Culture'. Virgin Atlantic website. Available at: http://careersuk.virgin-atlantic.com/life-at-virgin-atlantic/culture.html (accessed on 15 April 2014).

West MA, Dawson JF, Topakas A (2011). *NHS staff management and health service quality: results from the NHS Staff Survey and Related Data.* London: Department of Health. Available at: www.dh.gov.uk/health/2011/08/nhs-staff-management/ (accessed on 16 April 2014).

West MA (2012). *Effective teamwork: practical lessons from organizational research*, 3rd ed. Oxford: Blackwell Publishing.

About the authors

Michael West joined The King's Fund as a Senior Fellow in November 2013. He is Professor of Work and Organisational Psychology at Lancaster University Management School, Senior Research Fellow at The Work Foundation and Emeritus Professor at Aston University. He was formerly Executive Dean of Aston Business School.

He graduated from the University of Wales in 1973 and received his PhD in 1977. He has authored, edited and co-edited 20 books and has published more than 200 articles for scientific and practitioner publications, as well as chapters in scholarly books. He is a Fellow of the British Psychological Society, the American Psychological Association (APA), the APA Society for Industrial/Organisational Psychology, the Higher Education Academy, the International Association of Applied Psychologists and the British Academy of Management. He is a Chartered Fellow of the Chartered Institute of Personnel and Development.

Michael is an Academician of the Academy of Social Sciences. His areas of research interest are organisational cultures, collective leadership, team and organisational innovation and effectiveness, particularly in relation to the organisation of health services. He lectures widely, both nationally and internationally, on the results of his research and on his solutions for developing effective and innovative organisations.

Regina Eckert is a Senior Research Associate at the Center for Creative Leadership (CCL) and is the representative of CCL's research in the Europe, Middle East and Africa (EMEA) region. She is a scientist–practitioner and applies her research knowledge and findings in customised leadership programmes for diversity, women in leadership, and global top-talent development for clients across the region.

Gina uses her knowledge and research experience in developing cross-cultural leadership, especially in the EMEA region, and uses a range of methodical approaches to answer questions about leaders' career development, leadership and gender, globally responsible leadership, and leadership challenges around the world. She has managed the development of Global6, a new 360-degree feedback tool for global leadership.

Before joining CCL, Gina has consulted on quality management in German health care, on organisational change, and leadership development in the automotive industry. She holds a degree in psychology from the University of Munich, Germany, and a PhD in management from Aston Business School, United Kingdom.

Katy Steward is an Assistant Director in Leadership Development at The King's Fund. She joined the Fund in 2006 and has more than 20 years' experience of working in the public and private sector. Before joining the Fund she worked at Monitor on governance and leadership as Head of Governance Policy.

Katy has worked extensively in change management and organisational effectiveness. She has a PhD in engagement, culture and communication and following this worked as a consultant at KPMG, and was Vice President at Citigroup. She has implemented new structures, teams and processes, working at board level and below to define roles, change strategies, and develop leaders and cultures. Before coming to the NHS she worked for two years on government change programmes, including with the House of Commons and with the University for Industry.

She is a qualified coach and enjoys running action learning sets. She has a strong interest in board leadership and its impact on culture and governance. At The King's Fund she directs the Board Leadership programme and works with boards she set up with the Foundation Trust Governors Association. She also runs the New Medical Director programme.

Bill Pasmore joined the Center for Creative Leadership in 2008 and as Senior Vice President and Organisational Practice Lead, he leads CCL's efforts to help clients develop leadership strategies that their organisations can use to transform their leadership cultures and capabilities.

Before joining CCL, Bill was a partner in the corporate learning and organisational development practice of the consulting firm Oliver Wyman Delta. While there, he also headed the global research practice and worked with top executives of Fortune 500 companies on organisational architecture and development as well as succession planning, talent management, and strategic planning.

From 1976 to 1997, Bill was a tenured full professor in the Weatherhead School of Management at Case Western Reserve University, where he taught courses in the school's MBA and PhD programmes. He also headed his own consulting firm, Pasmore & Associates, which offered public workshops on large-scale change. He co-founded the Social Innovations in Global Management programme, which provides leadership and managerial training to socially responsible not-for-profit organisations around the world.

The King's Fund is an independent charity working to improve health and health care in England. We help to shape policy and practice through research and analysis; develop individuals, teams and organisations; promote understanding of the health and social care system; and bring people together to learn, share knowledge and debate. Our vision is that the best possible care is available to all.

www.kingsfund.org.uk   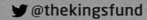 @thekingsfund

Published by
The King's Fund
11-13 Cavendish Square
London W1G 0AN
Tel: 020 7307 2568
Fax: 020 7307 2801

Email:
publications@kingsfund.org.uk

www.kingsfund.org.uk

© The King's Fund 2014

First published 2014 by
The King's Fund

Charity registration number:
1126980

All rights reserved, including
the right of reproduction in
whole or in part in any form

ISBN: 978 1 909029 31 6

A catalogue record for this
publication is available from
the British Library

Edited by Anna Brown

Typeset by Peter Powell

Printed in the UK by
The King's Fund